MANAGING YOUR TIME

Iain Maitland

Iain Maitland is an author and lecturer specialising in key management issues.
He has written more than 20 books, including *Getting a Result* and *Motivating
People* for the Institute of Personnel and Development.

Training Extras is a comprehensive series covering all the crucial management skill areas. Each booklet includes the key issues, helpful starting-points, and practical advice in a concise and lively style. Together they form an accessible library reflecting current best practice – ideal for study or quick reference.

Other titles in the series include:

Asking Questions Ian MacKay

Businesslike Budgeting Eric Parsloe and Raymond Wright

Customer Care Roland and Frances Bee

Listening Skills Ian MacKay

The Manager as Coach and Mentor Eric Parsloe

Motivating People Iain Maitland

Negotiating, Persuading and Influencing Alan Fowler

The Selection Interview Penny Hackett

Working in Teams Alison Hardingham

The Institute of Personnel and Development is the leading publisher of books and reports for personnel and training professionals and students and for all those concerned with the effective management and development of people at work. For full details of all our titles please telephone the Publishing Department at IPD House.

MANAGING
YOUR TIME

Iain Maitland

INSTITUTE OF PERSONNEL AND DEVELOPMENT

Typesetting by The Midlands Book Typesetting Company, Loughborough
Printed in Great Britain by
Short Run Press, Exeter

British Library Cataloguing in Publication Data
A catalogue record for this book is available from the
British Library

ISBN 0-85292-584-0 (pack of five)

The views expressed in this book are the author's own and
may not necessarily reflect those of the IPD.

INSTITUTE OF PERSONNEL
AND DEVELOPMENT

IPD House, Camp Road, London SW19 4UX
Registered office as above. Registered Charity No. 1038333
A company limited by guarantee. Registered in England No. 2931892

Contents

1

Introducing Time Management

What exactly is time management? To begin with it may be sensible to define this key subject and outline its component parts before going on to look at the likely benefits and difficulties that could arise when you are trying to manage your time successfully.

Defining time management

Time management may be defined quite simply as a system for controlling and using time as efficiently and as effectively as possible. Of course there is more to it than this brief definition suggests – a system must be geared to an individual's particular needs. One system cannot possibly suit everyone. Also, it should be loose and flexible so that it can be adjusted according to ever-changing circumstances.

Time is limited, transitory and fleeting – and therefore hard to control. Almost inevitably, you will feel you have too little time available today, but (just) enough tomorrow. Yet tomorrow always seems to be as busy when it arrives. If you can identify and eliminate (or at least much reduce) time-wasting activities, however, you will go some way towards controlling time itself.

Time is also difficult to use efficiently and effectively. It means working hard *and* well so that tasks are completed and results achieved on time – and first time. It is important to bear in mind that your time management system does not – or certainly should not – act in isolation. You can free more of your time by passing on activities to a junior employee – good for you perhaps, but not necessarily so for him or her!

Ideally, time management must be a unified, overall approach rather than a mixture of separate ideas, tactics and 'tricks of the trade'. It should encompass and affect all aspects of your work *and* at all times, while constantly being amended and updated to take account of the developing situation. Never expect to achieve perfection – although excellence *is* achievable, or significant improvements at the very least.

The components of time management

It is helpful to be aware of what a time management system might consist of, even though each person's approach will differ according to his or her individual circumstances. Typically, the introduction of a system would involve these particular stages:

- analysing your workload
- getting organised
- delegating successfully
- tackling paperwork
- handling meetings
- controlling time-wasting activities
- making the most of free time.

Analysing your workload

Initially, you must make sure that you know your personal, departmental and organisational objectives so that you are conscious of what you are doing, and where you are going. Compile a time log showing how you currently spend your time over a given period. Assess this time to judge whether you are using it wisely and well, and to spot where improvements could be made.

Getting organised

Next, it is sensible to prioritise your tasks according to importance and urgency. You may want to use a diary system to record your planned activities over the coming days, weeks and months. You might also wish to compose lists to remind you, and to check and monitor your progress.

Delegating successfully

Delegation has a key role to play in time management – after all, other people may be able to do a variety of jobs as well as, if not better than, you, thus saving your valuable time. You need to understand it thoroughly – both the benefits and the drawbacks. If appropriate, you should allocate selected activities to certain employees as and when required. You may have to overcome particular problems to ensure that these are completed properly, and on schedule.

Tackling paperwork

Paperwork can be a real time-waster, and a serious threat to the running of your system. You should arrange your workspace so that paperwork is handled efficiently. It is important that you know how to write and read effectively too, so that correspondence is dealt with as rapidly as possible. It is also a good idea to know when to pick up the telephone instead of writing or reading.

Handling meetings

You should be familiar with the do's and don't's of socialising with colleagues – for example, do be polite and friendly, but don't waste time chatting aimlessly in corridors. You have to be able to deal competently with informal meetings, perhaps during coffee or lunch breaks. Just as significantly, you need to be ready to face up to formal meetings, within your department and with superiors.

Controlling time-wasting activities

There are many time-wasting activities of which you have to be conscious, and for which you have to be prepared. Most notably, you must be capable of coping with interruptions, whether personal or by telephone. You may occasionally be called upon to solve other people's problems – do so as quickly and efficiently as you can. Many of these time-wasters can be controlled simply by being assertive – a core skill that you need to acquire as this system develops.

Making the most of free time

If – or when – your time management system is successful, you may find that you gain some spare time, often at the beginning or end of the day. You should think about how you can gainfully use this time. It is also important that you learn to relax and enjoy your leisure hours. Having worked hard and well, you deserve a rest and need to refresh yourself so that you will be ready to return to work, and to give one hundred per cent again.

The benefits of time management

Developing a winning time management system offers many benefits, in particular those listed below:

- greater control
- improved productivity

- increased free time
- higher visibility.

Conversely, a poor system or the complete absence altogether of a system produces the opposite effects.

Greater control

Clear objectives, prioritised and carefully planned tasks, the use of diaries and lists, and so on – all will help you to know precisely what you are doing, when, why, how, and for how long. As a consequence, you control and direct time, rather than the other way around. You are in charge, dictating what happens and when.

Improved productivity

Delegating certain tasks to appropriate colleagues, having a fuller understanding of how to handle time-consuming matters such as paper-work and meetings, and to control wasteful activities like gossip and telephone interruptions should ensure that work-rate and performance improves. Hopefully, tasks will be done both faster and better, leading to first-rate productivity within the firm.

Increased free time

A thorough reorganisation of your workload, the delegation of some tasks to selected employees, and the elimination (or reduction) of wasteful activities should lower the demands upon you, so freeing part of your time. Less pressure and stress, and a chance to relax (however briefly) can help to re-charge you – and must obviously have a knock-on effect on your work. After all, only a fit, healthy *and* refreshed individual can return to work hard and well, and make full use of all his or her time.

Higher visibility

Without doubt, a time-oriented individual – in control, efficient and effective, always raring to go – is more noticeable to his or her peers. Your superiors may well also perceive there to be some difference between you and any of your colleagues who are continually behind schedule, ploughing through overdue paperwork, and missing deadlines – a difference that may stand you in good stead as and when transfer and promotion opportunities arise.

The difficulties of time management

Inevitably, the implementation of a time management system is not easy. The practicalities of analysing your workload, getting organised, delegating, and so forth, are difficult in themselves, especially if you have not focused fully on such activities before. In addition, there are other obstacles that have to be faced, notably

- attitudes
- habits
- workload
- organisational culture.

Attitudes

If a successful system is to be developed, it often requires an almost total change in attitude by the individual, a complete re-evaluation of everything that has gone before – which may include an acceptance that performance to date has been poor or even a complete failure in some respects. Objectives may need to be set for the first time, tasks and time-scales re-appraised, working practices changed – all with regard to time management. Saving and making the best possible use of time has to become a priority.

Habits

The expression 'old habits die hard' is an apt one, especially in relation to time management. A system should not only apply universally but be ongoing as well. More often than not, bad habits tend to resurface after a while. Memories are relied upon rather than diaries and checklists, complicated paperwork is left until tomorrow, and coffee breaks become longer again. New – and time-oriented – habits must be developed and adhered to.

Workload

Sometimes a person's workload seems to be so heavy, diverse and incessant that for it to be restructured within a time management system appears impossible. All of the work is urgent and important; the diary is always full; no one can do the job quite as well, can complete so much of the paperwork, can attend so many meetings, and so on. But no matter what the nature and level of the workload may be, the development of an appropriate system *will* improve the situation.

Organisational culture

The way in which the organisation is structured and run can often be a problem for a time-conscious manager. Perhaps he or she has to work as part of a team, and is dependent on others' completing their tasks before his or her activities can be finished. Possibly, tasks are not foreseeable and cannot be scheduled until the last moment, and/or unexpected changes have to be made continually, all of which makes planning difficult – but never impossible, if a relevant system is in place.

Further reading

FORSYTH P. *First Things First*. London, Pitman, 1994
SCOTT M. *Time Management*. London, Century Business, 1992

2

 Analysing Your Workload

The first stage in the development of a successful time management system is to analyse your workload in relation to the time available to you. This analysis involves three key activities: knowing your objectives, compiling a time log, and assessing your time.

Knowing your objectives

It is important that you are aware of the objectives towards which you are working. Much of time management is concerned with making decisions – what and what not to do, which tasks should be carried out first, which ones can be delegated, and so on. Clear, concise objectives provide you with a framework in which to make these choices correctly.

Obviously, objectives – whether individual, departmental or organisational – vary from one situation to another. But they should all be

- specific
- realistic
- timed
- measurable.

Specific

You need to know exactly what you are supposed to be doing and where you are going. What is your precise role? What are your tasks and duties? What are the aims of your department? What is the organisation trying to achieve? Ideally, you should also know how you should be completing activities, *and* why. The greater your level of understanding, the easier it is to make accurate, time management decisions.

Realistic

Objectives must be attainable too – by you, by your department, and by the organisation itself. They must also be consistent with the resources that are available, including time. For example, there is little point in wanting to hold regular daily meetings unless everyone has the time to attend them. Individual, departmental and organisational objectives should all fit together and complement each other. Otherwise there is a conflict of interests, which makes decision-making that much harder, if not impossible.

Timed

You should know when various tasks and duties need to be carried out and completed, *and* have target dates for the achievement of overall objectives. This clearly helps to put everything into perspective, and creates a sense of order that will be of benefit as and when your time management system is being developed and subsequently refined.

Measurable

Objectives must be subject to some form of scale so that you can see if they have been achieved fully and on time – or, if appropriate, how far adrift you are from them. Enough details should have been provided about the objectives for you to measure your performance yourself. Objectives should be stated in quantitative terms – to produce so many units in a given time, to sell a certain amount over a specific period – because this makes it simpler to judge success or failure.

Compiling a time log

Conscious of this framework of objectives to work within and towards, you can move on to piece together a time log, which sets out the time you have and what you are doing with it. You cannot make improvements and build up a winning time management system until you know how well you are using it at any one moment. Compiling a time log consists of several steps:

- estimating work-time ratios
- dividing up time
- recording activities.

Estimating work-time ratios

Start by thinking about how you spend your time now, asking yourself various questions – and answering them truthfully. How many hours do I work in total? What activities do I do? How long do I spend on each activity? What do I spend most of my time doing? What do I spend the least amount of time on? Are these in proportion to the importance of the activities? Convert the times spent on each activity into percentage terms and show them on a pie chart for easy reference, as in Figure 1 below. (Simply multiply each activity's percentage by 3.6 to obtain the correct number of degrees in the chart.)

Figure 1
HOW SALESPEOPLE THINK THEY SPEND THEIR DAY

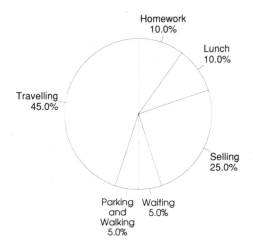

Even now, you may already have some ideas of areas for improvement – if not, you may be in for a shock! To help you to focus your attention more fully, take a look at the questions listed in the Questionnaire on page 10. If you are able to answer positively to any of them, you can almost certainly make better use of your time than you are doing at present. If your answers are all negative, have another look *after* you have completed your time log. By then, you may have changed your mind.

Dividing up time
It is sensible to consider how your time is spent over a period of perhaps two to four weeks (the longer the assessment, the more accurate your findings are likely to be). Using a chart such as the one shown in Figure 2, separate out each day into 15- or 30-minute segments, depending on whether you do a large number of short tasks or a smaller number of lengthier activities.

QUESTIONNAIRE: HOW ARE YOU SPENDING YOUR TIME?

Answer the following questions by ticking an appropriate box. Then decide if you need a time management system!

	Never	Sometimes	Often	Always
Do you do pleasant tasks first?	❏	❏	❏	❏
Do you do unpleasant activities last?	❏	❏	❏	❏
Do you need more time to complete your work?	❏	❏	❏	❏
Do you move from one task to another and back again?	❏	❏	❏	❏
Do you miss deadlines?	❏	❏	❏	❏
Do you find yourself doing tasks at short notice?	❏	❏	❏	❏
Do you have to deal with crises?	❏	❏	❏	❏
Do you like taking on new tasks?	❏	❏	❏	❏
Do you find yourself doing other people's work?	❏	❏	❏	❏
Do you prefer to do something yourself rather than pass it on?	❏	❏	❏	❏
Do you like to be involved with everything?	❏	❏	❏	❏
Is your desk cluttered and untidy?	❏	❏	❏	❏
Do you spend time searching for key information?	❏	❏	❏	❏
Do you put off paperwork until tomorrow?	❏	❏	❏	❏
Do you spend time chatting with colleagues?	❏	❏	❏	❏
Do people call in to see you unannounced?	❏	❏	❏	❏
Do you attend meetings?	❏	❏	❏	❏
Do you feel meetings could achieve more?	❏	❏	❏	❏
Do colleagues interrupt your work?	❏	❏	❏	❏
Does the telephone interrupt you?	❏	❏	❏	❏
Do people bring their problems to you?	❏	❏	❏	❏
Do you have to arrive early or stay late to complete everything?	❏	❏	❏	❏
Do you have little time to yourself during the day?	❏	❏	❏	❏
Are you stressed out and unable to relax?	❏	❏	❏	❏

Figure 2
TIME LOG

NAME:	DATE:
8.00	
9.00	
10.00	
11.00	
12.00	
1.00	
2.00	
3.00	
4.00	
5.00	
6.00	

ADDITIONAL COMMENTS _____

_____

_____

_____

_____

Recording activities

Get into the habit of spending a few moments at the end of every hour noting exactly what you did in the preceding two or four segments, as appropriate. You may find it simpler to record codes for each particular activity – T for travelling, P for paperwork, Tb for tea breaks, L for lunch, and so forth. Try to note down everything – including I's for interruptions! Establish a routine of making notes regularly rather than relying on your memory later on, for that may prove selective and inaccurate.

Assessing your time

After two to four weeks you should be able to sit down and look back over your completed time log to see exactly how that time has been used. Again, this activity can be divided up into three different steps:

- calculating work-time ratios
- identifying time-oriented tasks
- recognising time-wasting activities

Calculating work-time ratios

Reviewing your time, you should add up the precise number of hours worked. Is the total more or less than expected? Then put together a full list of all your activities, totting up the time spent on each of them. Is the total as anticipated? Convert these times into percentages and transfer them onto another pie chart, as in Figure 3. Compare your

Figure 3
HOW SALESPEOPLE ACTUALLY SPEND THEIR DAY

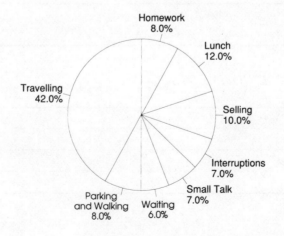

two pie charts. Are they similar, or not? Perhaps do a third pie chart, showing how you would *like* it to look. Is this achievable?

Identifying time-oriented tasks

If this 'ideal' chart is to achieved in real life – or at least worked towards – you will have to examine the tasks you are doing at the moment. Consider which ones can or should only be completed by you. Those that require specialist knowledge, or are concerned with confidential matters, perhaps? What else? Those that are new and untried, possibly? Others that involve disciplining members of staff or handling grievances? Thinking about these tasks, decide which ones seem already to be being done in a quick and efficient manner, and cannot be improved in any way. Are you absolutely sure? Contemplate over which ones might perhaps be performed faster and better, trying to work out what you would need to do to ensure this. How much can you improve things, and how long will these tasks then take to be completed?

Recognising time-wasting activities

It is wise to look closely at those tasks that you are currently carrying out and which could be classified as time-wasting activities. Identify tasks which are urgent and/or important, but which could be done equally well by someone else, such as an assistant or junior employee. Should you re-allocate these, and so free your time? Recognise those activities that are out-and-out time-wasters – gossipy chats, overlong tea breaks, and the like. You should try to reduce these to the minimum amount of time possible, but do not expect to eliminate them altogether. See which ones can be classified as 'time-oriented' and 'time-wasting', according to your situation.

Further reading

CAMPBELL A, DEVINE M. and YOUNG D. *A Sense of Mission*. London, Pitman, 1993
RABEY G.P. *In Charge*. London, Pitman, 1994

3

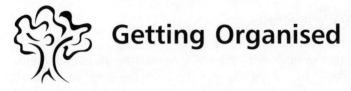 **Getting Organised**

Prioritising tasks

Having analysed your workload fully and thoroughly, you can move on and get yourself organised. To do this properly, you need to prioritise the tasks that you will be carrying out personally, and think about the possibility of using a diary system and composing lists to provide additional assistance as and when necessary. In prioritising there are three considerations:

- urgent activities
- important activities
- the urgency-importance ratio.

Urgent activities

Composing a lengthy list of *all* your activities, you should be able to put a mark (*U*) alongside those which need to be done as a matter of some urgency. For example, it may be urgent that you deal with a customer's telephone call immediately, or return it as promptly as possible. You might find it helpful to grade each of these tasks on a scale of 1 to 5, 5 being the most urgent.

Important activities

Similarly, you can then work through that same list of your tasks, placing marks (*I*) next to those activities which are of some importance. As an example, it may be important that you complete a report about a recent training programme you attended. Again, you could find it useful to classify each activity on a scale of 1 to 5, with 5 as the most important.

The urgency–importance ratio

It can be advantageous at this point to place your activities on a 'priorities axis' such as the one shown in Figure 4. Those put in the top right segment are both very urgent and very important, and should be done first. At bottom right, tasks are very important but not urgent, which suggests they come second. Activities in the top left section are not important but *are* very urgent, and you may want to do these third. Finally, tasks at bottom left are neither important nor urgent, so do them last of all.

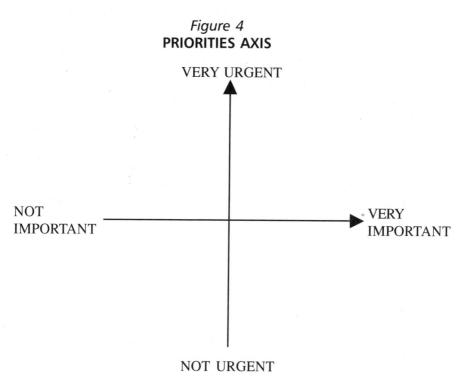

Figure 4
PRIORITIES AXIS

Using a diary system

A diary system plays a key role in effective time management, for success depends largely upon planning your work, and then working that plan! Given the individual nature of your activities, you should create your own unique system, employing various items, as listed below.

- wall charts
- diaries
- sticky labels.

You should also be aware of the dangers of utilising such a system, to make sure that you avoid them.

Wall charts

You will need to be able to take a (relatively) long-term view of your coming workload, over six months or, preferably, one year. Naturally, what you know of your precise work activities during this period of time will be rather hazy, but you should be able to make a note of major projects and their start and completion dates, one-off events such as conferences, the closure periods at Christmas and New Year, and non-work times including family holidays. You may find it easiest to do this on a wall chart, using colour-coded stickers and/or pins, as appropriate.

Such a broad outline will clearly help you to spot opportunities and to recognise potential problems *before* they occur. The prospect of an additional project may arise, for example, and by studying the chart you may be able to calculate how it might be manoeuvred into the schedule, although your first instinct might have been to reject it. In addition, work to be completed in six or nine months may require some tasks to be carried out immediately if it is to be done successfully. For example, invitations should be sent off well in advance of a conference. Without the constant reminder of a wall chart, you could overlook such activities until it is just too late.

Diaries

It is sensible to have a master desk diary – possibly supported by pocket diaries for yourself and any assistant (as long as they are all co-ordinated) – in which data can be recorded. Information should be as detailed as possible – who, what, when, where, why, how – because it is often difficult to remember precisely what you agreed to do now, at a later date. Note down everything in pencil, so that it can be changed, if or when required. Check the diaries regularly.

Sticky labels

You will almost certainly find it helpful to have a plentiful supply of sticky labels (such as 3M's 'Post-it' notes) close at hand, on which you can scribble notes, reminders, and so on. Immediately afterwards they can be stuck on to the wall chart or into your desk or pocket diary, and then be referred to and perhaps written up formally at a later, more convenient, moment, if still relevant.

Avoiding the dangers

Wall charts, desk and pocket diaries, and sticky labels can all assist you in building up a winning time management system – but you must be careful. It is easy to become over-dependent on them, to the point where you feel like having a nervous breakdown if any are misplaced! Make certain that they aid but do not *control* you. It is also tempting to become so involved with colouring in wall charts, filling in desk diaries, and so forth, that you do not do much else. You can waste time planning what you are going to do instead of actually doing it. Note it down quickly – then get on with your work!

Composing lists

It can be useful to draft daily checklists to help you through each day's workload in a smooth and efficient manner. You should approach these lists in three steps, which can be headed

- the night before
- the day itself
- the morning after.

The night before

Compose a checklist of the following day's activities at the close of the working day. Using a form similar to the one shown in Figure 5, jot down any definite meetings, interviews, appointments and the like, and their start and expected finish times. Alongside these, make a note of any other tasks that ought to be performed – such as report reading, letter writing and telephone calls – divided perhaps into two or three categories, typically 'musts', 'shoulds' and 'maybes' according to their order of urgency or importance. The next morning you can check your list again, to make sure you still agree and are happy with it.

The day itself

You should work through your 'To do' list one activity at a time, starting with the most urgent/important and going downwards from there. Attempt to concentrate fully on that one task, doing it as fast and as well as you can, rather than flitting from one to another and doing all of them at a substandard level. Mark off each activity as it is completed, and try not to return to it. Slot in any new tasks that arise during the day according to how urgent and/or important they are.

Figure 5
'TO DO' LIST

NAME:	DATE:	'TO DO TODAY' ACTIVITIES
		MUSTS
		SHOULDS
		MAYBES

8.00
9.00
10.00
11.00
12.00
1.00
2.00
3.00
4.00
5.00
6.00

ADDITIONAL COMMENTS _____

The morning after

At the end of the day – or at the very latest on the morning after – review what you have done, and prepare a checklist for the next day. You really ought not to be carrying forward any of the 'musts' or 'shoulds', for that would indicate that you are either overestimating how much you can do in a day or are not managing your time well enough. Some of the 'maybes' could be moved on, but try to give them a higher priority during the following day to avoid their staying stuck in that position until you suddenly realise they should have been done weeks ago!

Further hints and dangers

As with wall charts and diaries, you may find it beneficial to use some of those yellow 'Post-it' notes when compiling your lists. They are especially helpful when new tasks crop up during the day. Jot down a comment on one of your sticky labels and then attend to it in due course.

Again, be careful not to become over-reliant on lists. At all costs, avoid doing nothing all day but composing lists, re-arranging them, and then changing them back later on. It makes you look and feel busy – but you're not really doing anything worthwhile!

Further reading

TREACY D. *Clear Your Desk*. London, Century Business, 1991
LAMBERT T. *Key Management Tools*. London, Pitman, 1993

4

 Delegating Successfully

Delegation is a key ingredient of an effective time management system. You must understand delegation so that you know when (and when not) to hand over tasks to colleagues, such as junior employees. You also need to know how to allocate activities, and overcome related problems that may arise.

Understanding delegation

A clear and straightforward definition of delegation is that it is 'the process of passing certain tasks and duties from one person to another, typically a superior to a subordinate. The delegate receives sufficient authority to complete the work satisfactorily, although the delegator retains overall responsibility for its success or failure.' A fuller picture of delegation can be created by contemplating its

- advantages
- disadvantages.

Advantages

Obviously, delegating work to others will free part of your time, so allowing you to concentrate your skills and efforts on more urgent and/or important matters. It should also develop your subordinates' capabilities, increasing their confidence and stature, and providing greater job satisfaction. New ideas and approaches to old methods may be found too. It can build morale, and motivate everyone within the team, if they know that you are willing to give them room to grow, be more successful and progress.

Disadvantages

Most of the drawbacks of delegation arise simply because it is not done wholeheartedly, or properly. Most notably, the delegator hands over work but not authority, because he or she is frightened of letting go. Perhaps he or she will not be needed any more. Possibly the delegate will do a faster and better job. So the delegator constantly interferes and checks what is being done, creating ill-feeling and wasting (two people's) time. Often only the dullest or the most unpleasant tasks are passed on, which again causes resentment. Also, the delegator sometimes chooses the wrong employees to do the activities – whoever is close at hand may be given the work regardless of whether or not he or she is capable and willing. The questionnaire below may help you to judge if you are delegating well or not.

QUESTIONNAIRE: ARE YOU DELEGATING WELL?

Tackle these questions carefully, ticking the appropriate box. Your answers may indicate if you are a successful delegator or not.

	Never	Sometimes	Often	Always
Do you think your subordinates lack ability?	❏	❏	❏	❏
Do you believe it is quicker to do everything yourself?	❏	❏	❏	❏
Do you worry that a colleague may do a faster or better job?	❏	❏	❏	❏
Do you like to be seen as overworked?	❏	❏	❏	❏
Are you reluctant to hand over tasks?	❏	❏	❏	❏
Do you just pass on routine activities?	❏	❏	❏	❏
Do you only ever hand over unpleasant work?	❏	❏	❏	❏
Do you keep the most enjoyable tasks for yourself?	❏	❏	❏	❏
Do you delegate activities to the nearest subordinate?	❏	❏	❏	❏
Do you tell delegates to report back only on completion of a task?	❏	❏	❏	❏
Do you instruct delegates to report back every step of the way?	❏	❏	❏	❏
Do you continually check up on delegates?	❏	❏	❏	❏
Do you completely ignore delegates once a task has been handed over?	❏	❏	❏	❏
Do delegates ask you what they are supposed to be doing?	❏	❏	❏	❏
Do delegates get angry with you?	❏	❏	❏	❏

	Never	Sometimes	Often	Always
Are delegated tasks left unfinished?	❑	❑	❑	❑
Do you have to complete delegated activities?	❑	❑	❑	❑
Do you forget about delegated work upon completion?	❑	❑	❑	❑

Allocating activities

To avoid the potential disadvantages of delegation, it is vital that considerable thought and attention is given to the allocation of activities. Various areas must be examined, in particular:

- the activities delegated
- the time
- the delegate.

The activities delegated

You should think carefully about the tasks that you are going to delegate. There are no hard and fast rules about this because it depends largely upon individual circumstances. Write out a list of your tasks and then decide for yourself which ones should or should not be delegated at this time. Ideally, those activities that are being passed on ought to be complete ones with some responsibilities attached to them, ones that will use and build on the delegate's abilities, and have clear criteria against which progress can be measured.

Always try to avoid handing over new tasks in circumstances where successful work practices have not yet been fully implemented. Similarly, do not delegate activities central to your job, such as those that involve planning or developing confidential ideas. Delicate and/or contentious issues (such as disciplinary and grievance procedures) should be retained by you. As important – if not more so – is *never* to hand over all the really boring and mundane tasks that you dislike intensely, for the delegate will loathe them too, and loathe *you* as well.

The time

Not surprisingly, time is a key factor when choosing which activities to delegate. You evidently want to spend more of your valuable time on the most important tasks, and less on the least important ones. It is therefore sensible to delegate those parts of your work which tend to be time-consuming but not especially important. Do be aware that time does not always favour delegation. For example, urgent matters must be dealt with *now* rather than later. There may not be enough time to instruct, explain, check that everything is understood, and so on – so this is an occasion to get on and do it yourself, and quickly!

The delegate

You must be absolutely certain that the person to whom you are delegating activities is a suitable delegate. He or she should have many attributes, not least an understanding of departmental and organisational objectives, the skills, knowledge and experience to do the work, and the self-confidence and desire to do it. With regard to time management, make sure that he or she has the time available – remember, your system should not operate alone. You should not simply dump excess tasks on others who may be equally busy. The questionnaire below will help you to decide whether the person is likely to be acceptable or not.

QUESTIONNAIRE: WOULD HE/SHE MAKE A GOOD DELEGATE?

Take a look at the following questions. You should be able to answer 'yes' to all of them. If you cannot, the person may not be the ideal delegate on this occasion.

	Yes	No
Does he/she fully understand departmental and organisational objectives?	❑	❑
Does he/she have the skills needed to do the job properly, and on schedule?	❑	❑
Has this or a similar activity been carried out before by him/her?	❑	❑
Do you know his/her strengths and weaknesses?	❑	❑
Are you confident that he/she can make a success of it?	❑	❑
Is he/she confident enough to do the job?	❑	❑
Does he/she want to do it?	❑	❑
Will the activity fit comfortably into his/her schedule?	❑	❑
Will he/she follow set procedures?	❑	❑
Will he/she learn from the experience?	❑	❑
Will it benefit you and/or others in the team?	❑	❑

Overcoming problems

By far the easiest way of overcoming problems is to act before, rather than reacting after, they have occurred. Do this simply by approaching the whole process of delegation in the correct manner, thus reducing the likelihood of difficulties arising at all. Four main steps can be identified here:

- instructing clearly
- retaining control
- staying in touch
- evaluating results.

Instructing clearly

Make certain that the delegate is able to get it right first time – nothing wastes time more than having to do something again. Help to ensure this by telling him or her what needs to be done exactly, why, and by when. Support verbal comments with written instructions, as necessary. How a particular task should be done can be outlined if appropriate but not too rigidly, because that would stifle initiative and originality. Obtain feedback to check that all is understood fully. Be sure that his or her colleagues know what is happening too, and that they accept it.

Retaining control

Delegation does not mean handing over a task and then ignoring what happens. After all, you still have overall responsibility – as your line manager will be quick to remind you if something goes wrong. So avoid the 'Tell me about it later' approach when delegating work. At the other extreme, steer clear of the 'Don't do anything until you've checked with me' attitude because this breeds frustration and ill-will on the part of the delegate. Strike a happy medium – perhaps a 'Keep me informed regularly, letting me know if or when I can help you' style.

Staying in touch

Introduce these checks at the beginning, making sure that they are known and agreed before the delegate commences work. Mentioned and/or incorporated later, they could create the impression that you have lost confidence in him or her, with the knock-on effect of damaging morale. Sprung upon him or her without prior agreement, such checks may cause a resentful and hostile atmosphere to develop which could stop the work being completed well and punctually. Although constructive advice may be welcomed during these regular checks, try not to interfere at other times. Be around, though, to help if necessary, on request.

Evaluating results

It is imperative that you *and* the delegate review the process at set stages, and upon completion. Think about the activity. Was it done satisfactorily, and on schedule? Have systems been improved, or new approaches developed, even? Consider the delegate. Has he or she gained from the experience? Increased skills, perhaps? Boosted confidence? Contemplate his or her colleagues. Has the effect of delegation been positive or negative? Do *they* now want to take on more? Were there any problems? If so, what, and why? What can you do to get it right next time?

Further reading

OATES D. *Leadership: the Art of Delegation*. London, Century Business, 1993
PAYNE J. and S. *Letting Go without Losing Control*. London, Pitman in association with the Institute of Management, 1994

5

Tackling Paperwork

Paperwork is a major part of many jobs nowadays, and can have a significantly adverse effect on time management unless it is controlled carefully. To exert control, you must arrange your workspace well, and know how to read and write efficiently. Sometimes it can be more sensible to pick up the telephone instead of writing, so you have to ensure that you can do this effectively too.

Arranging your workspace

Your working area must be arranged in a user-friendly way (as far as possible) so that you can make the most efficient and effective use of your time. More specifically, you should think about

- layout
- organisation
- health and safety.

Layout

Ideally, your workspace should be laid out so that the equipment, machinery and materials you use most often are to hand. You may find it helpful to list various items in order of usage and then set them out in order within your 'perfect' working area. Obviously, it is not always possible to have everything near by – the company photocopier is unlikely to be relocated to suit your personal preferences, for example. In such instances, try to batch together those activities which involve the photocopier (or whatever) and attend to them all at the same time. In this way you only have to walk up three flights of stairs once, rather than on four, five or six (time-consuming) occasions.

Organisation

You must endeavour to keep your desk clear and tidy at all times, retaining in front of you only those papers that are relevant to the immediate task in hand. Everything else should be put into 'In' and 'Out' trays, files, desk tidiers, and the like. This will enable you to concentrate exclusively on the work you are doing. A cluttered and disorganised desk may make it hard for you to pick out what you need quickly, and could even lead to your feeling permanently tense and stressed out, as you sense you are losing control. You will be!

Health and safety

Your workspace must be safe and hygienic if you are to work hard and well, completing activities successfully and on time. A bright and ventilated office is a pleasant environment to work in and encourages you to get on with your tasks. In dark and musty surroundings you will be ill at ease and distracted, which means you will work less well. It could even lead to accidents and illness – and time off work is wholly wasted. The questionnaire below may enable you to assess whether you are in a safe, healthy environment. If not, try to get it changed for the better!

QUESTIONNAIRE: IS THIS A SAFE AND HEALTHY ENVIRONMENT?

If you can tick the 'Yes' box to all of these questions, you are probably working in a safe and healthy workplace. If not, you should be seeking improvements.

	Yes	Sometimes	No
Are the seats and benches comfortable?	❑	❑	❑
Can equipment and machinery be operated comfortably?	❑	❑	❑
Can you move about easily?	❑	❑	❑
Are floors, gangways and ramps clear, even, clean, and non-slippery?	❑	❑	❑
Are steps, corners and obstacles marked clearly?	❑	❑	❑
Are floor openings covered or guarded?	❑	❑	❑
Are toilets clean, ventilated, accessible, and in working order?	❑	❑	❑
Are wash-basins available with hot and cold running water, soap, towels, and other cleaning items?	❑	❑	❑

	Yes	Sometimes	No
Is any eating and drinking area for the staff pleasant and well equipped?	❑	❑	❑
Are lockers or hanging spaces available for clothes and bags?	❑	❑	❑
Is the temperature comfortable everywhere?	❑	❑	❑
Is suitable work clothing provided, when appropriate?	❑	❑	❑
Is heating equipment in safe working order?	❑	❑	❑
Are all areas well ventilated?	❑	❑	❑
Are the premises comfortably illuminated?	❑	❑	❑
Is there sufficient emergency lighting available, if necessary?	❑	❑	❑
Are outside areas lit at night?	❑	❑	❑
Are windows and lights clean?	❑	❑	❑
Are equipment, machinery and processes quiet?	❑	❑	❑
Is a quiet area available between working times?	❑	❑	❑
Are noisy areas, machinery and processes identified with warning signs?	❑	❑	❑
Do you know how to operate equipment and machinery safely?	❑	❑	❑
Are safe work systems and procedures adhered to at all times?	❑	❑	❑
Is safety equipment supplied, as required?	❑	❑	❑
Are machinery and accessories kept in good working order?	❑	❑	❑
Does everyone know what to do in an emergency?	❑	❑	❑
Do emergency procedures work in practice?	❑	❑	❑
Is a fully stocked first-aid box available?	❑	❑	❑
Are the premises secured against vandals and burglars?	❑	❑	❑
Do procedures exist to protect everyone against aggressive customers?	❑	❑	❑

Reading effectively

It is important that you are able to deal efficiently with the numerous memos, reports, faxes, letters, and other documents that come onto your desk, day in and day out. Probably the most time-effective way of doing this is for you (or an assistant) to prioritise all incoming paperwork into the following categories:

- action
- information
- disposal

They can then be dealt with accordingly.

Action

Those papers that can be read and dealt with fully by you personally *and* now should be given your complete and immediate attention. Go through each paper highlighting key points with a marker pen and making relevant notes. This approach will help to stop you having to read the same document twice, and waste your time. Try not to 'speed read' through – simply picking out (what appear to be) the main points – because this is risky: you could make mistakes. Do not file the paper until you have taken whatever is the appropriate action – perhaps to draft a reply, or to chase an overdue payment.

There will be some paperwork that you cannot deal with personally and/or now. Perhaps a superior needs to make a final decision, or further information is required before the document can be processed. But the issue remains an important one, and still needs your prompt attention. Possibly, you should forward it to a colleague, simply adding an explanatory comment to the bottom before passing it on, which saves time. Alternatively, you may have to put it into a 'Pending' file with a note attached stating when it should be looked at again – ideally as soon as that further information has been obtained. Jot down a reminder in your weekly or monthly diary, if relevant.

Information

Much of the paperwork you have to handle will probably have been provided for reference purposes only, such as minutes of meetings you have attended and copies of memos and reports which are of limited direct interest to you. Nonetheless, check through them carefully, highlighting any significant areas and making notes as appropriate, prior to filing or handing them over promptly, as relevant. To maintain a fluid (and therefore time-friendly) filing system, it is a good idea to put on each document a 'disposal date' when they can be checked and – if no longer worth retaining – thrown away. If papers are being passed on, attach your comments to them rather than generating a fresh memo: this saves everyone's time and money.

Disposal

Some papers that land on your desk may not really merit your attention at all, such as sales brochures and the like. On the other hand, you may *want* to read up about the latest car accessory or computer software – but don't do it now, though! Save your precious time for more urgent and/or important matters, leaving that literature until your own free time.

Writing efficiently

Equally significantly, it is crucial for you to be able to write memos, reports, and so forth in an efficient way. To do this successfully you need to work swiftly through five steps:

- knowing your goals
- establishing facts
- analysing the recipient
- preparing a draft
- completing the document.

Knowing your goals

Begin by identifying what it is you want to achieve with this memorandum, letter, or whatever – perhaps to confirm that you have read a particular report, or to chase up an outstanding bill. Always have your aim focused clearly in your mind – what you have to state develops from this. It can also help you to decide whether you should write, or whether you should perhaps telephone instead. Do you want a clear, written record, or would you prefer a more immediate and personal approach, with the chance to discuss certain points?

Establishing facts

Be sure that you are wholly familiar with the facts of the matter, making certain you really have read (the relevant parts of) that report, or know when the invoice was issued, due to be paid, pursued before, and so forth. Then make a rough-and-ready note of everything and anything that might need to be included in your correspondence. Do not worry too much about its layout, order and phrasing at the moment – just concentrate on putting down whatever comes into your mind. At this stage, it is better to have something irrelevant left in than something relevant left out.

Analysing the recipient

You should be confident that the message you want to put over will be understood by the recipient and not misinterpreted in any way, for that would generate additional time-wasting correspondence. A clear message may also help to elicit the required response – the remittance of a cheque, or whatever. Try to take into account the personality of the person who is to read your comments, and his or her knowledge and views of the subject you are writing about. Put yourself in his or her position, imagining what the reaction to your communication is most likely to be.

Preparing a draft

Knowing what you want to achieve, conscious of the facts, and taking account of who is to be the recipient, you should certainly be able to compose a draft. Sketch out – as appropriate – the main and subheadings in logical order, and/or the key points you wish to make in the most relevant sequence. Delete any that no longer seem significant – these will often become apparent as you progress. You may wish to compile several drafts before settling on a fairly complete text that can be fitted into your organisation's standard format for memoranda, letters, and so on.

Completing the document

It is worth while spending a little time on improving your text. Check spelling, punctuation and grammar, for (even minor) errors can cause confusion. Keep words and sentences short and simple so they are easy to read and understand. Otherwise you may have to spend extra time later on explaining what you meant. Avoid technical language and jargon *unless* you are writing to an expert who may feel patronised if you use simplified words – arguments take up time too! Cut, cut, and cut again, to ensure it is concise and to the point. State it once, move on, finish. Then get rid of the document as fast as you can.

Picking up the telephone

Your phone can be a real time-saver, often allowing you to communicate in a quicker and more personal way than a written communication can do. It nevertheless needs to be handled wisely. In the wrong hands it can use up even more of your time. Your approach should in many respects be similar to writing a memo or letter: you must know your goals, establish the facts, take the recipient into account, and prepare a draft of what you want to say or ask. There are other points worth bearing in mind as well, including

- grouping your calls
- being prompt
- timing yourself.

Grouping your calls

Try to get into the habit of saving up all your calls and making them at the same time (unless of course, not making one *now* will hold up urgent/and or important work). Calls here, there, and everywhere tend to fragment and disrupt the day, breaking into ongoing activities and disturbing your concentration. Avoid calling at the beginning of the day because some people will be unavailable, which wastes your time (and money). Similarly, steer clear of lunch-time and the end of the day. Late morning or mid-afternoon may be best, because most people tend to be available and receptive then.

Being prompt

'Say what you have to say, and shut up!' should be your motto when speaking on the telephone. You should have prepared a draft of the key points you want to make, and any questions you wish to have answered, which should enable you to work through the conversation quickly and efficiently. Keep your introduction to a bare minimum – say who you are and why you have called. Then press ahead, dealing with one point at a time, and in succession. Do not be distracted. If the recipient's attention begins to wander, bring it back with a polite comment such as 'Thank you, can I now ask you about . . .?' or something similar. Finish as soon as you possibly can – and go on to the next call on your list.

Timing yourself

It is surprising how much additional time can be used up when telephoning people – lines are engaged, you are put on hold for a few minutes, the person is not in but will ring back, and so forth – and then you spend several minutes waiting for that return call which is not made. Monitor your use of the telephone over a period of time – if you have not already done so – and try to gauge how the total call-time breaks down between 'talking' and 'non-talking' time. You may be shocked to discover precisely how much of your valuable time is wasted in this way.

Endeavour to cut back your 'non-talking' time as far as possible. You will never eliminate it completely, but you should be able to reduce it to a minimal amount. If one is available, store regularly dialled numbers in the telephone's memory; this can save you a few moments – as can a re-dial facility. It all adds up! If the phone has a built-in loudspeaker, it will make it easier for you to keep working while you are on hold. In addition, *force* yourself to concentrate on work when waiting for a call to be returned.

Further reading

TREACY D. *Conquering the Paper Mountain*. London, Century Business, 1994
COCHRANE P. *The Power of the Phone*. London, Pitman in association with the Institute of Management, 1993
WAINWRIGHT G.R. *Tricky Business Letters*. Pitman in association with the Institute of Management, 1993

6

Handling Meetings

Like paperwork, meetings are a major user – and potential abuser – of time. Much of your working day and week will be taken up with various types of meeting, both informal and formal ones. It is important that you are able to socialise with colleagues wisely and well, and can deal with informal meetings and face up to more formal ones, perhaps with heads of departments.

Socialising with colleagues

Getting on with your associates is absolutely essential, in business and in personal terms – you *need* to talk, discuss commercial matters, converse, develop friendships, and the like. Nonetheless, you should think carefully about the time spent on chatting, laughing, drinking and eating with your colleagues – too long, and it cuts into your valuable working time. If you have not yet done so, calculate how much of your time is taken up socialising. Reduce it by concentrating on the two areas which encourage it to excess:

- times
- places.

Times

Inevitably, there are certain times of the day when it is tempting to chat longer than you should do: on arrival in the morning when some people are keen to discuss the previous evening's (or weekend's) activities; during coffee, lunch and tea breaks; and at the end of the day, when others are willing the clock to strike five-thirty. You have clearly to be especially disciplined and focused on time management at these moments, so that you adhere to your planned schedule. Make sure you take (the agreed time for) breaks, though, both regularly and often. They refresh and rejuvenate you, allowing you to return to your tasks with a clear head and fresh ideas.

Places

Equally significantly, there are some places where you can often be persuaded to stop for a chat, or to linger rather longer than you ought to – perhaps in the corridor, by the vending machine, near the photocopier, or in reception, typically. Again, you need to be aware of this, and either try to avoid such locations completely or visit them once instead of the usual two or three times. Concentrate on being time-conscious when you are there, perhaps setting a time limit. Challenge yourself to set a reduced time limit for each occasion.

Dealing with informal meetings

Some of your time may well be allocated to various informal one-to-one meetings – such as appraisal and counselling interviews with subordinates and superiors, and appointments to view new product lines with sales agents. Not surprisingly, these can be quite diverse by nature, and should be approached on an individual basis. Several common features nonetheless exist, as far as time management is concerned:

- before
- during
- after.

Before

It is important that all meetings, however informal they may be, are timetabled carefully into your monthly and weekly diaries, as appropriate. Unscheduled, they will wholly disrupt your system. Make sure that you allow enough time for appointments. It is probably better to overestimate slightly and find yourself with time left over for completing short, minor tasks, rather than to attempt to cram in as many as possible and leave yourself racing furiously against the clock. Include start and anticipated end times, making certain that you adhere to them to remain on course.

During

You can help yourself to keep on schedule by deciding beforehand exactly what you want to cover, and in which order. It can be beneficial to compile a plan of points you want to cover, or questions you wish to ask. An appraisal form, sales literature, or other relevant documents might be helpful because they suggest a framework around which you can develop questions and points. Stick closely to the plan, making sure you return to it if or when any other person deviates from it. Refer regularly to the passing time to show it is important – 'Let's wrap this up in ten minutes', 'We must be moving on', and so forth. Brief an assistant or a colleague to come in towards the end, which should give you the opportunity to round everything up on time.

After

It can be a good idea to include short 'buffer' periods of five minutes or so between successive appointments to allow you to make notes of any action that needs to be taken, of further appointments which should be added to your diary, and so on. It will also enable you to have a coffee, visit the loo, or simply stretch your legs, refreshing you and improving your concentration for the next one. Without these buffers, you may find that your appointments begin to run into each other, and you soon fall behind schedule.

Facing up to formal meetings

Without doubt, pre-scheduled, formal meetings such as the monthly, departmental one are excessive users of time – before, during, and after they have been held. Whether you are responsible for organising and/or attending them regularly, you must try to ensure that they are always

- organised properly
- chaired well
- attended positively.

Organised properly

A meeting must be planned carefully if it is to be effective and time-efficient. Why is it being held? It must be staged for a specific reason, not simply because one is traditionally held at that time. You should consider the alternatives – perhaps reading a departmental report would be just as effective, but less time-consuming. What are its objectives? It is important that only a limited number of topics are covered, so that attention can be concentrated fully, over a short but intense period of time.

Who should attend the meeting? Only those who really have something to say and/or learn. If you do not, stay away, and just study the subsequent minutes of the meeting. When should it be staged? Ideally, at a convenient time for all concerned. It ought to be subject to mutual agreement and scheduled in everyone's diaries well in advance. Where should it be held? Again, somewhere convenient, as well as comfortable and free from interruptions.

An agenda should be provided for all participants, and circulated to them some 24 to 48 hours before the meeting begins. This document must set out the purpose of the meeting along with its date, start and finish times. It is sensible to commence a meeting relatively close to a tea or coffee break, lunch, or the end of the day, because it provides a natural incentive to conclude punctually. The venue, the names of participants, and the topics for discussion (possibly with their approximate timings) should be incorporated too. Avoid rounding off with 'Any other business' because it invites time-wasters to witter on endlessly about their personal grievances.

Chaired well

Much of the effectiveness and efficiency of a formal meeting depends upon the skills of the chairperson – who may be you, on occasions, now or in the future. He or she should begin by setting out the purpose and objectives, prior to going on to work through the points on the agenda in sequence. Each topic should be outlined before being opened up to comments from all participants. It is important that the chair, without being too domineering or making judgements, encourages all relevant parties to speak. He or she needs to ensure that speakers do not meander or ramble, and should summarise the main points and what has been agreed at the end of each topic, and at the close of the meeting itself. Take a look at the questionnaire below to see if you are a good chairperson.

QUESTIONNAIRE: ARE YOU A GOOD CHAIRPERSON?

Answering these questions honestly by ticking the appropriate boxes may indicate how good you are as a chairperson, and could suggest areas for improvement.

	Yes	No
Are you always well prepared?	❏	❏
Do you study key documents?	❏	❏
Do you check that facilities are satisfactory?	❏	❏
Do you see that equipment is working?	❏	❏
Do you make sure minutes are taken?	❏	❏
Do you ensure that the meeting starts on time?	❏	❏

	Yes	No
Are the objectives spelt out by you?	❏	❏
Is the agenda referred to?	❏	❏
Are the rules established by you?	❏	❏
Do you introduce everyone, if necessary?	❏	❏
Do you lead the meeting?	❏	❏
Is the meeting controlled by you?	❏	❏
Do you ask questions to clarify matters?	❏	❏
Do you make sure everyone contributes?	❏	❏
Are time-wasters cut short by you?	❏	❏
Do you watch the clock, reminding people of the time?	❏	❏
Do you summarise, clearly and regularly?	❏	❏
Do you keep to the timings of the agenda?	❏	❏
Do you ensure that decisions are reached?	❏	❏
Is a full but brief conclusion provided by you?	❏	❏
Do you make sure the meeting finishes on time?	❏	❏
Do you check that follow-up action is taken?	❏	❏
Do you read the minutes?	❏	❏

Attended positively

Alternatively, you may simply be expected to go along to the meeting – although you should really attend only if you can contribute to or benefit from it. Perhaps just one part of the meeting is relevant – if so, attend for just that! Study the agenda beforehand, working through it carefully to plan out what you need to say on, or find out about, each topic. Be clear and concise when you speak – and quiet if you have nothing to say! Listen carefully, and make notes if you are learning something new. Aim to go in and come out as swiftly as you can. The questionnaire on page 39 may help you to work out if you are a good attender or not.

Minutes should be typed up and distributed to participants and other interested parties within 24 to 48 hours of the meeting. These should state the date, time, and location of the meeting, along with the names of the attendants, and include apologies from those who were obliged to be absent. It should then spell out the topics discussed, with any conclusions and decisions made, and actions planned. The date, time, and location of the next meeting may then be added, if relevant. Another meeting should be scheduled if – and only if – it serves a specific purpose, not because it is part of a routine process.

QUESTIONNAIRE: ARE YOU A GOOD ATTENDER?

If you can tick the 'Yes' box to all of these questions, you are a good attender at meetings. If not, there may be room for you to improve your performance.

	Yes	No
Do you prepare thoroughly?	❏	❏
Are the necessary documents read beforehand?	❏	❏
Do you know how to use the equipment?	❏	❏
Do you tell colleagues not to interrupt you?	❏	❏
Do you arrive on time?	❏	❏
Are mobile phones and bleepers turned off?	❏	❏
Are pens and notepads brought in with you?	❏	❏
Do you speak clearly and concisely?	❏	❏
Do you listen carefully to what others have to say?	❏	❏
Do you avoid interrupting people?	❏	❏
Do you ask questions to verify matters?	❏	❏
Are all of your comments directed through the chairperson?	❏	❏
Do you write notes, where appropriate?	❏	❏
Do you avoid being distracted at all times?	❏	❏
Do you carry out all actions, as agreed and punctually?	❏	❏
Do you look through the minutes afterwards?	❏	❏

Further reading

HODGSON P. and J. *Effective Meetings*. London, Century Business, 1992

MARTIN D. *Manipulating Meetings*. London, Pitman in association with the Institute of Management, 1994

SHARMAN D. *The Perfect Meeting*. London, Century Business, 1993

7

Controlling Time-wasting Activities

It is essential that you are able to control any time-wasting activities that can disrupt your carefully designed time management system. In particular, you need to know how to cope with interruptions and how to solve other people's problems (which will inevitably be brought to you from time to time). You can often deal with these various time-consuming activities simply by being assertive, as and when necessary.

Coping with interruptions

You should try to minimise interruptions as far as possible, so that you can concentrate fully on the tasks in hand. Not only does each interruption use up several minutes of your time but there is a knock-on effect on your work. It will take you a few minutes on each occasion to re-focus on what you were previously doing. Interruptions can be classified in three main ways:

- by personal contact
- by telephone
- by oneself.

By personal contact

Many interruptions are by other members of staff – superiors, colleagues and subordinates. Endeavour to reduce these by making appointments to see people at set times, and telling them not to interrupt you, at least not during certain periods. Put up a 'Do not Disturb' sign to remind them! If appropriate, ask an assistant to put off callers by saying you are in a meeting, on the telephone, or similar, and promising to pass a message on. You can then decide what needs pursuing. Some tasks will have to be dealt with fairly promptly, although others will simply disappear, because they were not urgent or important after all. When necessary, slip off to an empty room where you can hide away, and finish off top-priority work.

If you are interrupted, impose a time limit on the exchange by stating 'I've got five minutes', or something of the sort – and make sure you adhere to it. Do not invite the person to sit down because it encourages conversation; remain standing yourself, if possible. Keep to the point at all times, avoiding small talk and meandering onto other topics. Without being rude, signal that your time is limited – 'One more thing before we finish.' Glance at your watch or a clock if necessary, or train an assistant to interrupt with an 'urgent message', if all else fails. End as quickly and politely as you can.

By telephone

Similarly, the telephone is a great invader of time. If relevant, an assistant or colleague can screen calls, only putting through the most urgent and/or important ones, the rest being returned by you in one go, later on. When necessary, set aside times when you must not be disturbed at all, guaranteeing this by switching on an answerphone or even unplugging the telephone. Try to stop friends and family ringing up for chats or to ask you to pick up a pint of milk on the way home. If interrupted, adopt a comparable approach to personal callers – set a time limit, keep to the point, and so on.

By oneself

Perhaps surprisingly, *you* could be the biggest cause of interruptions to your work. Like everyone else, you are probably flattered that a colleague is seeking your advice or a sales representative wishes to sell something to you personally. Maybe you are currently working on tasks that you dislike, so that you positively welcome interruptions – and if nothing interrupts you, you'll give yourself another break by making yet another cup of tea or having a look at a different piece of paper. Anything, rather than do the work in front of you.

The questionnaire on page 42 will help you to decide if you are your own worst enemy in this area, if you are not already aware of the answer. If you are susceptible to interruptions, then you need to work hard at concentrating wholly and exclusively on the immediate task. Hide yourself somewhere; unplug the phone; keep away from the coffee machine; and just take that one sheet of paper with you. See if you can attend to it in a set time – and reward yourself with that coffee, if successful.

QUESTIONNAIRE: ARE YOU WASTING YOUR OWN TIME?

Have a look at these questions to see if you are a time-waster!
Which boxes you tick should highlight your bad habits. Try to get rid of them!

	Never	Sometimes	Often	Always
Do you find yourself rearranging your desk and then changing it back again?	❏	❏	❏	❏
Do you amend your 'To do' list, without actually doing the tasks on it?	❏	❏	❏	❏
Do you sit and think about what you will do tomorrow, in the middle of today?	❏	❏	❏	❏
Do you re-read papers in case you might have missed something important?	❏	❏	❏	❏
Do you rewrite letters, worrying about their exact phrasing?	❏	❏	❏	❏
Do you re-run conversations in your head to make sure you said everything?	❏	❏	❏	❏
Do you wait for a colleague to return with a document, rather than getting on with something in the meantime?	❏	❏	❏	❏
Do you wait for a telephone call to be returned, doing nothing else until it has?	❏	❏	❏	❏
Are you continually making cups of tea?	❏	❏	❏	❏
Are you constantly going to the toilet?	❏	❏	❏	❏
Do you watch other people work?	❏	❏	❏	❏
Do you stare into space?	❏	❏	❏	❏
Do you watch raindrops running down the window pane?	❏	❏	❏	❏
Do you deliberately waste time?	❏	❏	❏	❏

Solving other people's problems

Too many managers and supervisors spend their precious time dealing with the problems encountered by their colleagues and subordinates – and as a consequence, they manage your time, instead of you! You must avoid becoming involved in their workload and worries as far as you can, or you will find it means you have to fit extra tasks into your already full schedule. It also does not benefit your staff if you are always solving their difficulties. They will never develop and progress if you do everything for them. In general, adopt the following procedure:

- spot the problem
- pinpoint the options
- offer the solution.

Spot the problem

When a person approaches you with a problem, you should begin by asking him or her to identify exactly what it is. Perhaps he or she doesn't know how to handle a particular customer, or isn't sure how to compose a certain letter. Encourage your colleagues to tell you what they have done so far to solve their problems. They may not have done anything at all, automatically turning to you for assistance, so by asking them this you will be forcing them to focus upon what they should already have done. Make them think for themselves, instead of simply doing it for them.

Pinpoint the options

Likewise, get them to contemplate the alternatives available to them – to say this to the customer or that, to put this into the letter, or something else. 'What do *you* think you should do? ... What else? Is there anything else *you* can think of?' Hopefully, questions such as these – which turn the problem and its remedy back towards the person – will enable them to decide precisely what they should do to resolve the difficulty, and why.

Offer the solution

If necessary – but only as a last resort – you should offer suggestions about how how they might solve the problem. It is clearly better if you can assist them to find their own solution because that will build up their confidence and skills, making it less likely that they will turn immediately to you next time. Obviously, it is tempting to just give them the answer straight away to save your time now, but this will tie up more of it later on when they come back again and again. Spend a few extra minutes with them now, so that they will be encouraged to sort themselves out in future.

Being assertive

To cope with personal and telephone interruptions successfully, and to solve other people's problems in the most effective way, you will often need to be assertive – to stand up for yourself in a firm yet polite manner. This is not always easy, but these guidelines may help you to improve your approach:

- just say 'No'
- say 'Yes' later.

Just say 'No'

You *must* be prepared to say 'No' – or even 'NO!' – as and when necessary, most notably for trivial matters, and when you are too busy with urgent and/or important issues to speak to that junior, take that sales agent's call, or whatever. You have the right to use this word – so say it promptly and firmly. Point to that 'Do not Disturb' sign to emphasise it, if need be! Concentrate on what you are doing, so that the task is completed properly and on time.

Say 'Yes' later

It is wise to strike a balance, though. If your door is permanently closed and you continually say 'No', people will eventually stop knocking and asking altogether – and you may miss out on crucial information, and find yourself excluded from work relationships and teams. So make certain you are accessible at key times, that you return telephone calls as promised, and so on. You want to be seen as firm but fair – agreeable and helpful – but definitely not a soft touch.

Further reading

DE LA BEDOYERE Q. *Managing People and Problems*. Aldershot, Gower, 1988

BIRD, P. *Tame that Phone!* Corby, Institute of Management, 1994

8

Making the Most of Free Time

The introduction and ongoing development of a successful time management system should have many benefits, not least a greater control over your own affairs and improved productivity for your organisation. Probably the most noticeable change, though, will be that you gain spare time, and it is sensible to consider how you can make the most of this. It is also wise to think about your leisure time, ensuring that you enjoy it, so you return feeling fresh and ready to work hard and well.

Gaining spare time

Your improved management of time – by getting organised, delegating more, reading and writing efficiently, and so on – may well mean that you find yourself with the occasional free moment now and then throughout the day. Perhaps the easiest way of looking at and deciding what to do with these is to divide the day into three, separate sections:

- the beginning
- the middle
- the end.

The beginning

The beginning of the day – from when you wake up to when you start work – often offers the best possible opportunity for you to improve your use of time, and to prepare yourself well for the day ahead. Washing, eating, exercising, and dressing are all fairly routine matters which enable you to think, to plan, and to work through the issues of the coming day in your mind. Perhaps you can rejig the planned order of activities into a more efficient sequence, or rehearse what you are going to say to a visiting salesperson. Travelling can seem to be a waste of time, but you could read a report or write a letter while on a train, or practise your introductory comments as chairperson of a formal meeting while you are driving in.

The middle

A manager or supervisor who has recently implemented a time management system soon finds that he or she acquires five minutes here and there during the day. Typically, meetings end more punctually than before, and tasks are completed quicker than expected because fewer interruptions now occur. It may be a good idea to use these times to deal with the 'maybes' on your daily checklist – especially those that have been there for several days, or even longer. Alternatively, why not tidy your desk, cleaning up cups and plates? Read those 'disposal' papers which are about to be thrown away? Visit the photocopier while it is quiet and you can avoid time-consuming chats? Anything that is more worthwhile than staring into space!

The end

That last part of the day when the clock ticks from five o'clock to five past, then ten, and agonisingly slowly towards fifteen can be the most productive of the time-oriented day. Review the day's activities. Did you complete *all* of the 'musts' and 'shoulds' on your list? If not, why not? Perhaps you were overambitious, misjudged the time required, or were distracted. What do you need to do to improve? Piece together tomorrow's 'To do' list, taking account of what happened today. Then, mull it over in the car or on the train home until it is to your satisfaction. The questionnaire below may enable you to decide how well you are using your travelling time.

QUESTIONNAIRE: DO YOU MAKE THE BEST USE OF YOUR TRAVELLING TIME?

How often do you do the following tasks when travelling to and from work? Your answers, as ticked in the appropriate boxes, may help to show how you can employ your travelling time more effectively.

	Never	Sometimes	Often	Always
thinking about work	❑	❑	❑	❑
reading documents	❑	❑	❑	❑
writing documents	❑	❑	❑	❑
telephoning people	❑	❑	❑	❑
rehearsing conversations	❑	❑	❑	❑
discussing work with colleagues	❑	❑	❑	❑
other work-related activities	❑	❑	❑	❑

Enjoying your leisure time

It is imperative that you are able to switch off at the end of each day, and enjoy your free time. Too often the demands of the job may spill over into the evenings and weekends so that you find yourself either doing additional work or worrying about it. Clearly, you cannot expect to work effectively and efficiently on an ongoing basis unless you have regular breaks to refresh yourself. So you need to be capable of

- banishing stress
- becoming relaxed
- striking a balance.

Banishing stress

There are many causes of work-associated stress – most notably an excessive workload, poorly trained subordinates, having to work to deadlines, long working hours, attending meetings, and the effects of work on your private life. Not surprisingly, most of them are time-related. You may already be aware that you are suffering from stress because of these. Perhaps you are rushing to complete a report for the following morning's meeting, and have therefore brought it home with you. Sometimes you may not be fully aware that you are affected by stress, for the symptoms are not always obvious. Answering the questions in the questionnaire below might enable you to judge if you are a sufferer or not.

QUESTIONNAIRE: ARE YOU SUFFERING FROM STRESS?

Stress can show itself in a variety of ways – through behavioural, emotional and physical symptoms. Tick the 'Yes' box to any of these, and you may be a sufferer. See your doctor if symptoms are serious or continue for any length of time. Do not ignore them.

	Yes	No
Behavioural Symptoms		
Has the quality of your work worsened?	❏	❏
Has your output decreased?	❏	❏
Are you making mistakes at work?	❏	❏
Do you find it hard to reach decisions?	❏	❏
Are you complaining more than you used to do?	❏	❏
Are you drinking more?	❏	❏

	Yes	No
Are you eating more?	❑	❑
Have you lost your appetite?	❑	❑
Do you continually feel tired?	❑	❑
Do you find it difficult to get a good night's sleep?	❑	❑
Has your behaviour changed for the worse in any way?	❑	❑

Emotional Symptoms

	Yes	No
Do you have rapid mood changes?	❑	❑
Do you feel anxious?	❑	❑
Do you find yourself daydreaming?	❑	❑
Do you feel irritable much of the time?	❑	❑
Are you finding it hard to concentrate?	❑	❑
Do you feel detached from your colleagues?	❑	❑
Have you lost interest in them?	❑	❑

Physical Symptoms

	Yes	No
Do you often have headaches?	❑	❑
Are you continually sweating?	❑	❑
Do you have double vision?	❑	❑
Are you experiencing chest or back pains?	❑	❑
Do you sometimes find it difficult to breathe?	❑	❑
Do you often have indigestion?	❑	❑
Is your stomach constantly upset?	❑	❑
Do you sometimes feel sick?	❑	❑
Do you experience tingling sensations in your arms and legs?	❑	❑

If you are suffering, you should try to eliminate (or at least drastically reduce) the causes, as far as possible. You can do this by focusing even more fully on some of those key time management skills. Always prioritise, giving most time to the urgent/important tasks and least to the least significant ones. Give these the time they must have nonetheless, though, but no more. Continue to delegate, because this provides you with more time for the priorities. Communicate with your colleagues: get out of the office once in a while, but watch the time. A checklist of other ways of controlling stress is set out on page 49.

CHECKLIST OF WAYS TO CONTROL STRESS

Stress can be tackled in many ways, including the following ones. Do not hesitate to take medical advice, though, when appropriate.

- Work for no more than an absolute maximum of 10 hours each day – then switch off!
- Do not take on unrealistic deadlines. Be honest with yourself: many tasks can wait a little while.
- Force yourself to move at a slightly slower speed when you begin to feel rushed off your feet.
- Vary your routine occasionally. It will help you to view old tasks in a new light, and cheer you up.
- Congratulate yourself on completing an activity on time and/or well. Reward yourself, perhaps with a cup of tea and a biscuit!
- Try to support others and accept help from them. 'Being there' is important.
- Accept that you cannot change human nature, so do not get uptight about other people's attitudes.
- Forget about the past – the future is more significant. Concentrate on improving that.
- Smile more than before – it's infectious!
- Relax for 10 or 15 minutes every morning and afternoon. Go for a walk, or sit somewhere quietly. Shut your eyes, listen to music; do whatever calms you. Rejuvenate yourself.
- Take 30 minutes over lunch. Eat and drink slowly. Avoid talking about business. Turn off!
- Take at least one day off every week.

Becoming relaxed

Stress reveals itself in people by means of a variety of symptoms – including headaches, breathing difficulties and muscular pains. To deal with these emotional and physical symptoms, break free from work while you are at home. Build up your hobbies. These can absorb stress and frustration, and help to relax your mind. Take exercise – typically, little but often – although you should speak to your doctor before commencing a fitness programme; be careful that you do not overdo it.

Make sure that you eat sensibly too, steering clear of extreme and off-beat diets. Go for the consensus view, perhaps eating a little of everything, but nothing to excess. Similarly, make certain that you have enough sleep as well. Don't go to bed so late that you leave yourself tired in the morning. Find out what your ideal sleep time is through trial and error, and then try to stick to it as far as you can.

Striking a balance

Of course work is important, and the way you manage your time will have a huge impact on it, and on you too. Nonetheless, there has to be a balance between your working and your private lives. 'Word hard and play hard' is an old cliché but contains a key truth – if you work hard, you deserve to take it as easy as possible as well. If you put as much effort into enjoying your spare time, you will feel happier and relaxed, and will return to your job with the positive attitude you need to work effectively and efficiently, using your time to the best of your ability.

Further reading

CARTWRIGHT S. and COOPER C. *No Hassle!* London, Century Business, 1994
ADAMS J.D. *Stress, Health and Your Lifestyle*. London, Mercury Books, 1992